C000061035

Finding God
in Anxiety & Depression

by
Fr Antonio Ritaccio

*All booklets are published thanks to the
generous support of the members of the
Catholic Truth Society*

CATHOLIC TRUTH SOCIETY
PUBLISHERS TO THE HOLY SEE

All Scriptural quotations in this booklet are from the *Revised Standard Version*.

Image Credits

Page 4, *Contemplating the meaning of life.* © illustrissima/Shutterstock.com; Page 16, *Silhouette & Christian cross at railhead wooden bridge.* © Somrak Jendee/Shutterstock.com; Page 30, *The beach with footprints in the sand.* © Ozerov Alexander/Shutterstock.com; Page 42, *Station of the Cross, a man carries the cross towards the next station.* San Beda College, Manila. © Rainier Martin Ampongan/Shutterstock.com; Page 52, *Holding wooden cross and sunset sky.* © Seksun Guntanid/Shutterstock.com

ISBN 978 1 78469 193 6

Contents

God has a plan for your life! 5

Finding hope when faith is weak 17

When forgiveness is impossible. 29

When we don't have strength to carry the cross. . . . 41

Clinging to God in Prayer 53

Prayers. 69

    Useful resources. 78

    Bibliography 79

God has a plan for your life!

Anxiety and depression are the two most common mental health conditions in Britain today, yet sufferers can often feel ashamed of what they are going through because of the stigma attached to mental illness. Sometimes sufferers can be misunderstood and judged by others to be morally weak. Comments like "Try harder" or "Pull yourself together" can make things worse. For this reason, some people who live with anxiety, depression or both can be extremely good at hiding their condition. In a few cases, the consequences of pretending that everything is okay can be devastating. The 2004 document *Cherishing Life*, produced by the Bishops of England and Wales, states:

> Most if not all of us have to contend with illness at some time or other. Illness is an occasion of spiritual need. It provides a challenge to our faith, our hope and our love to remain able to appreciate life even in the midst of suffering. Particularly distressing

is the phenomenon of mental illness which may deprive someone of the ability to direct their own lives. People suffering from mental health problems will often isolate themselves, even seeking to end their lives violently. Many people experience depression to differing degrees, and some require intense medical treatment in hospital, prolonged psychotherapy, or life-long medication. The wider community has a responsibility to provide people who are ill with adequate and reliable support and access to the help they need. Neither mental or physical illness nor disability can strip people of their dignity as human beings, no matter how severe the condition.

Suffering from anxiety or depression is not merely a matter of feeling sad or worried. Most people will experience intense moments of sadness and worry at some stage in their lifetime while managing to get on with their everyday lives. However, for those who live with either or both of these medical conditions, the negative impact on every aspect of their life – the way they think and understand the world, their feelings, and their physical health – can be considerable. Anxiety and depression can affect anyone, at any age. Although they are different disorders, depression and anxiety can often have overlapping symptoms, such as tension, irritability, difficulty sleeping, poor appetite and inability to concentrate. Each condition is treated differently even though they are often experienced and referred to together.

Finding hope in anxiety and depression

Hope can make all the difference when it comes to living with mental illness. Without it, life becomes meaningless. If you experience particularly testing times with your condition, you might find it hard to believe that God has a plan of love for your life. The Church has always announced this fact: God knows you, and at the same time he searches for you. He knows you because he created you with a purpose. He searches for you because he respects your freedom to reject him. He will not impose himself on you without your permission. He longs for you to open your heart to him so that he can find a place there.

Perhaps you might ask: "If God loves me, then why is he allowing me to suffer?" There is no easy answer to this question. The question of suffering is a "mystery", a term which means that we can only understand it if God reveals its true meaning to us. God wants you to know his plan for your life so that you may have hope. But he is not happy to only reveal it to you from a distance. Instead, God chose another way, the way of compassion. By entering deeply into the human condition of suffering and death as a man, he became the companion of everyone who cries out "My God, my God, why hast thou forsaken me?" (*Ps* 22:1). When we consider the cross on which Jesus was crucified and died we can see that, through it, God does shed some light on all suffering: united with the cross of Jesus, we can now dare to hope that our own suffering and death is united with his Resurrection.

Today, God wants to accompany you. As you read this booklet, I invite you to pray. Ask God to reveal himself to you in a new way and to show you his plan for your life. Above all, it is important to know that your anxiety and depression is not a mark of failure. On the contrary: God identifies with your condition through the suffering of his Son Jesus, who endured his cross and his death as a sacrifice for our sins. Like everyone who suffers from mental illness, his mind was crucified with a crown of thorns. You can be confident in the knowledge that, in your pain, you are very close to the suffering heart of God. You are close to Christ's death and his Resurrection!

God's plan for your life

The details of God's plan for your life begin with the first book of the Bible, the Book of Genesis. It shows us that suffering was not part of God's original design for humanity. The first man and woman on earth,

Adam and Eve, were created with a unique place in God's creation. They were made in the image of God as individual persons sharing in God's divine life. They found their place at the heart of creation in the Garden of Eden, a place free from evil, suffering and death. We can imagine Adam walking with God in the cool of the day, both enjoying each other's company. God created everything for us, and so it is hard to understand why we don't always trust him.

We were made to serve and love God and to offer back to him everything that he has done for us. We are never happier than when we are in love with God, and unlike any other created thing, we are never more fully alive than when we make a gift of ourselves to others. In the beginning, Adam and Eve experienced perfect unity (communion) with each other and with God. Isolation, mistrust, confusion, anxiety, depression and death were never part of God's design.

Evil opposes God's plan

It was in the perfect paradise of Eden that evil first appeared through the "seductive voice" of a fallen angel: the devil. Also known as "Satan" or the "Ancient Serpent", he is behind the disobedience of Adam and Eve (cf. *Catechism of the Catholic Church* (*CCC*) 391-2). Angels were created naturally good by God but Satan, together with many others, freely chose to reject

God's authority and his plan. Driven by hatred for God, the Ancient Serpent knew how to wound God's heart: he led our first parents to disown God. They chose a life of independence from God, in the same way that a branch might separate itself from a tree; something very profound died in their soul on that day and they experienced fear and mistrust of God for the first time (*Gn* 3:1-13). Through their free choice, they lost sight of God's original plan of happiness and now found themselves isolated from each other and from God.

Since our first parents and the whole of creation are bound up with each other, the whole visible world was also affected; even the ground was now cursed (see *Gn* 3:17). Depression and anxiety became a reality, and all the descendants of Adam would lose sight of the Paradise they once had; but there is a word of hope: God admonished the serpent with the announcement that his deception would be defeated through the offspring of a woman: "I will put enmity between you and the woman, and between your seed and her seed; he shall bruise your head, and you shall bruise his heel" (*Gn* 3:15).

The Church sees in this promised "woman" the Blessed Virgin Mary, whose son, Jesus, would crush the head of the serpent. It is a promise that somehow lives in every person's heart, in the knowledge that we were not made for death but for eternal life.

God restores his plan

The voice of the seductive serpent continues to seduce us today. It does not speak to us when we are well. Instead, it waits to use our pain to tell us that life is not worth living. Fighting this oppressive voice is a daily battle for those who are at their wits' end, but Jesus shows us how to fight. He shows us the way in which we can overcome every trial.

At the start of his three-year ministry Jesus approaches John the Baptist for baptism in the Jordan River. Immediately after this, Jesus is led by the Spirit into the desert to be stripped of every possible support and consolation, and to then be tempted by the devil. His solitude in the dry, barren desert lasts for forty days (*Mt* 4:1-12). By being tempted after his long period of isolation from the world, he identifies with everyone who is attacked by Satan's lies in the midst of their depression and anxiety: the devil's first tactic is always to isolate us from God and from others. The devil presents Jesus with three temptations. However, they are really all the same one: the temptation to doubt God's love for him. Every one of these temptations is subtly designed to put Jesus's relationship with his Father into question. By prefacing the temptations with the statement "If you are the son of God" the devil tries to trick Jesus into doubting his relationship with his Father. It is the same trial that is put before us with every pain that we endure: we hear an inner voice asking the question "Where is God?" The devil tries to put before us the deception that God has abandoned us.

Jesus opposes the evil one's tactics in two ways: first, he stands firm in his identity: he is the beloved Son, with whom his Father is well pleased. He clearly heard this declaration at his baptism earlier; he knows with all his being that he is loved deeply:

> And when Jesus was baptised, he went up immediately from the water, and behold, the heavens were opened and he saw the Spirit of God descending like a dove, and alighting on him; and lo, a voice from heaven, saying, "This is my beloved Son, with whom I am well pleased." Then Jesus was led up by the Spirit into the wilderness to be tempted by the devil. (*Mt* 3:16-17, 4:1-11)

The Good News is that God the Father declares exactly the same intense love for all those who are baptised in his name! Christians become God's adopted children in baptism, and this is why the devil wants to steal this identity from them. For this reason, the second way in which Jesus defeats Satan's attacks is our greatest defence: simply not to engage with the devil but instead to proclaim the Word of God. The Scriptures were inspired by the same Spirit that cries out from the heart of a person "Abba! Father!" (*Ga* 4:6). When we pray with the Scriptures, we allow God himself to speak to us. Even if we don't always understand what we are reading the demons do! Against the temptation to doubt God's plan for our life, we can only win the battle by accepting the Good News of our identity.

Accepting the gospel requires repentance and faith. Faith is our response to God who reveals himself to us. To repent does not mean being disgusted with oneself. Instead, it means changing our mind about being separated from God and recognising that his loving power is greater than ours, and that he is on our side! God wants to help us to win the fight against anxiety and depression! It means turning our back on the deception and lie of Satan that God has rejected us and instead believing and accepting the power of Jesus Christ over our lives. We cannot be baptised or remain in baptism's grace without repentance and faith. In baptism, Christians are reborn as adopted children of God and, at the same time, the rebellious influence of the Ancient Serpent is broken. The gift of the Holy Spirit confirms us as members of the Kingdom of God; and, in the end, God will restore all things to himself:

At the end of time, the Kingdom of God will come in its fullness. After the universal judgement, the righteous will reign forever with Christ, glorified in body and soul. The universe itself will be renewed: The Church...will receive her perfection only in the glory of heaven, when will come the time of the renewal of all things. At that time, together with the human race, the universe itself, which is so closely related to man and which attains its destiny through him, will be perfectly re-established in Christ. (*CCC* 1042)

If you live with depression and anxiety, this Good News can give you hope to believe that God the Father has prepared for you a place in his Kingdom: Wait! Hope in the Lord! He is coming to get you!

Prayer

O Lord, I am lost. I am sorry that my love for you has grown cold. Please send your Spirit to me like the dewfall and ignite in my heart the fire of your love. Refresh in my mind what is anxious and renew in my soul what is lost. Console me with your divine presence, through Christ our Lord. Amen.

Tips for focusing on God's plan
for your life in anxiety and depression

- Keep a set of blank postcards on which to write brief scriptural passages from the Bible that speak to you about God's faithfulness. Use them as bookmarks or stick them in places where you will often see them. In times of doubt, the Word of God allows us to remain focused on the truth.

- Meditate on Jesus's Sermon on the Mount in Matthew's Gospel which puts our lives into the perspective of God's plan for us in his Kingdom (*Mt* 5:1-7:28).

- Draw inspiration and hope from the lives of the saints to see how God's plan unfolded in their lives. Become especially familiar with the lives of the saints represented at your parish church.

Finding hope when faith is weak

Sometimes it can be impossible to know that someone we see at work, in our church, or elsewhere is suffering from depression, because they may be hiding their condition so well. It may have taken incredible amounts of willpower and effort for them to get out of bed, to shower and to get ready to come out. We may be able to hide from each other, but God is always searching for us, even though no one can really hide from him.

In the Garden of Eden, Adam and Eve hid from God out of anxiety and fear of him. Nevertheless, God came looking for them. He called out to Adam, "Where are you?" (*Gn* 3:9). It is a question that God continues to ask each one of us every day. To come out of hiding means that we must stand before God without masks. It also means that we must be prepared to let go of our preconceived ideas about him (*CCC* 2779).

We tend to form impressions of God from our early childhood experiences of those in authority over us, especially our parents. Generally speaking, that is good, but we are also in danger of transferring our negative experiences of them on to God. In this sense, we can understand why he commands us to resist making up false images of him (see *Ex* 20:4).

Our self-image, too, is affected by the way our parents treated us: even if we were accepted and loved as children, just one traumatic experience of rejection can lead us to feel that we were not wanted, predisposing us to anxiety, depression or both. Ultimately our wounded self-image affects the way we relate to God as our Father. If our parents were strict, or absent, and so on, we can end up perceiving God as being a harsh lawmaker or indifferent to us, etc. In the end, we might conclude that there is something wrong with us, and find that all of our motivations in life are filtered through the lie that God will only accept us if we behave in a certain way.

God wants us to relate to him as he is in himself, and not as part of an image of him that we have constructed in our minds. For this reason, God has revealed himself to us by sending us his only Son as his ambassador – to give us hope in our exile and to let us see the true face of God and the heart of the Father.

Our encounter with God gives us hope

Having hope in the depths of depression or anxiety is not something which we can muster up by sheer willpower. It is a supernatural gift from God that comes from an encounter with him. He reveals himself to us especially through the announcement of the Good News of his saving power, known as the *Kerygma*. This message, proclaimed, carries a unique power to call us out from our hiding places. Like babies, smitten by their mother's smile, we are captivated by the truth, goodness and beauty of God's love. Our response is faith, and hope is born in us. Pope Benedict XVI tells us in his Encyclical, *Spe Salvi*, that the word "hope" is so central to biblical faith that in several passages the words "faith" and "hope" seem interchangeable.

When we hope for something, in some sense we then already possess it in the future. The God-given gift (theological virtue) of hope not only allows us to live out our present lives well amid our daily sufferings but it also "throws open the doors to the future for us". In the darkness and gloom of depression, hope is God's way of allowing his children to get a glimpse of his plan for their lives.

Pope Benedict points to St Josephine Bakhita as an example of what happens to a person when this encounter takes place for the first time in the midst of their suffering. Born around 1869 in Darfur in Sudan, Bakhita was kidnapped at the age of nine by slave-traders, and endured a terrible daily life of servitude and violent abuse from her masters.

Although no one had ever told her about God, in the darkest moments of her life, God communicated himself to her and gave her the supernatural gift of hope. Despite being the victim of unspeakably cruel treatment as a slave, she knew, at every level of her being, that she was loved by a creator God whom she could not see. This conviction gave her an inner freedom that her masters did not have. It gave her the power to forgive and even love those who abused her. It was this theological virtue that rescued her from a deeper slavery of despair. When she finally learnt about Jesus Christ and the Catholic faith, her convictions about God's love for her were confirmed. She was baptised and gave her life to the Lord as a religious sister.

St Bakhita's life shows us that it is possible to find God even in the midst of depression or anxiety: our suffering is transformed and it becomes rooted in hope. It allows us to persevere through pain as we strive towards the prize of heaven that awaits us. Searching for God through the heaviness that accompanies both anxiety and depression can lead a person to hope in God's plan of love for them.

Hope reveals the heart of the Father

It took the first followers of Jesus (the twelve Apostles) a while to finally understand that the mission of Jesus was not to sort out all of their problems but to reveal God the Father's heart to them. When Jesus taught them to pray to the Father, he did not show the Father to be an impatient, outraged God who is itching to send someone to hell. He gave them, instead, the confidence to share in his own intimacy with the Father as adopted children of God, by getting them to call God "Abba". On this basis, we can hope in his saving help in all our trials. Pope Benedict XVI tells us:

God is a Father who never abandons his children, a loving Father who supports, helps, welcomes, pardons and saves with a faithfulness that surpasses by far that of men and women, opening on to dimensions of eternity. "For his steadfast love endures forever", as Psalm 136 repeats in every verse, as in a litany, retracing the history of salvation. The love of God the Father never fails, he does not tire of us; it is a love that gives to the end, even to the sacrifice of his Son. Faith gives us this certainty which becomes a firm rock in the construction of our life: we can face all the moments of difficulty and danger, the experience of the darkness of despair in times of crisis and suffering, sustained by our trust that God does not forsake us and is always close in order to save us and lead us to eternal life. (Pope Benedict XVI, General Audience, Wednesday 30th January 2013)

It was this hope in the Father's mercy that transformed the Apostles from being horrified spectators of the Passion of Jesus to fearless preachers of the gospel. Like St Bakhita, they were changed by their encounter with the true face of God, after which they had the capacity to love everyone in the face of every suffering. They gave the ultimate witness by accepting death freely whilst forgiving those who martyred them, because in hope they were already risen with Christ: "If then you have been raised with Christ, seek the things that are above, where Christ is, seated at the right hand of God." (*Col* 3:1)

Hope gives meaning to our suffering. It is the road map that allows us to persevere on our pilgrim journey through life. When a person is lost in the depths of depression or the confusion of anxiety, hope makes it possible for them to get a glimpse of the plan God has for them. Fr Raniero Cantalamessa, the preacher to the papal household, describes the place which hope holds in our spiritual life:

A Christian wrote a poem on theological hope. He says that the three theological virtues [faith, hope and charity] are like three sisters: two of them are grown and the other is a small child. They go forward together hand in hand, with the child hope in the middle. Looking at them it would seem that the bigger ones are pulling the child but it is the other way round; it is the little girl who is pulling the two bigger ones. It is hope that pulls faith and charity. Without hope everything would stop. We can see this in our everyday lives. When a person reaches the point of having no hope in anything, it is as if he were dead. Often people even kill themselves or allow themselves to die slowly. Just as a person about to faint is quickly given something strong to drink or smell to revive them, so to those on the point of giving up the struggle, a reason to hope must be offered. They must be shown that they still have a chance so that they will take heart and start again. (Raniero Cantalamessa, *Life in Christ: The Spiritual Message of the Letter to the Romans*)

Hope gives light in darkness

Someone who finds themselves overwhelmed in the darkness of their mental health condition can easily be robbed of any hope as panic gives way to hopelessness. Anxiety can cause a person to fixate their attention on the immediate problem in front of them without thinking about the possibility that there might be a bigger picture. For example, when Joseph, the son of Jacob was sold into slavery by his brothers, his life seemed like it had come to a cruel end. Jacob was inconsolable when he heard the lie that his son had been killed by a wild animal (*Gn* 37:18ff). Yet, despite the apparent mess, God's master plan gradually unfolded as Joseph not only went on to save his brothers and his father from famine but also set in motion the events that would eventually lead to the Exodus and ultimately to the coming of Christ and our salvation, which we celebrate at every Mass.

The Church invites those suffering from an anxiety disorder or depression to trust that, in the apparent confusion and chaos of their experience, their lives are somehow an important part of the history of salvation. There is a well-known metaphor describing God's providence as a tapestry that has two sides. In the face of the problems of our lives, we are invited to reflect on which side of the design we are looking at:

> Life is like a piece of tapestry, one side bears a picture perfect in every detail, with colours of different light and shade blending in exquisite harmony. This is the finished picture of a life that has been well spent. It is the picture as we will see it in the world to come. For then and then only will we understand God's plan for us. The reverse side

of the tapestry represents life as we see it now. It is a picture of a confused mixture of threads and colours. There seems to be no purpose for this cutting or that knotting and for the apparent lack of planning. Yet the hand of the Master-Weaver is there, for every heartache, temptation, sorrow is there, in God's plan, to perfect us. A valuable piece of tapestry would take many, many years to bring to perfection. So God, in his infinite wisdom, takes a human lifetime to complete the tapestry of one life. (Rev. Bro. G B Sherriff, *Courage and a Man's Part*, 1965)

The Father delivers us from the darkness of evil

The stigma attached to depression and anxiety can easily cause anyone to lose hope and hide their condition, not just from God but also from others through a fear of rejection. Behind this fear is a deception that we are alone in the world. This lie is so powerful in our lives that only God can deliver us from it. The *Our Father* prayer contains the petition that we be delivered from all evil. To pray these words with confidence is to trust in the same power that delivered the Israelites from slavery in Egypt. Our enemy, the devil, is the father of lies. He is only interested in stealing from us our heavenly inheritance, killing us and destroying the work of God in us (see *Jn* 10:10).

Ultimately his influence is behind our fallen human condition which includes anxiety and depression. In the rite of baptism, the Church has given us the means to reclaim the ground we might have lost by exposing and renouncing the devil's influence over us. In the rite of Christian initiation for adults, candidates to be baptised are helped to progress in their spiritual journey by various minor exorcisms along the way.

On the night of the Easter Vigil, just before they are plunged into the regenerating waters of the font, they publicly reject Satan, and all his works, and all his empty promises (or "show"). After this lengthy process of breaking Satan's influence over them, they are then free to accept God as their Father as they are plunged three times into the waters of rebirth in the name of the Father and of the Son and of the Holy Spirit.

Whether we were baptised as adults or as infants, it is important to realise that we must face a daily struggle with temptations as the power and influence of evil is persistently trying to master us and take away our hope. As children of God, we can be confident in the power of Jesus Christ to win this battle for us when we remain close to him by renewing our baptismal vows every day in prayer.

Prayer

Heavenly Father, my hope is being teste[...]
for the times that I have not trusted yo[...]
for sending your Son, Jesus Christ, to s[...]
my sins. I accept him as my Lord and Saviour. Please
send your Holy Spirit to guide me and help me in my
search for you. Amen.

Tips for finding hope in anxiety and depression

- Keep a daily journal where you make a point of
  noting down at least five things that you are grateful
  for and bring these to prayer. Even if you find your
  list repeating itself every day, it is a way of knowing
  that God has not abandoned you. Bring your list
  of thanks to Mass and offer these up in your heart
  during Holy Communion.

- Join and commit to a prayer group where you
  can build up trusted friendships and benefit from
  mutual prayers and support. Ask for help to find
  one suitable for you from your parish priest or
  your diocesan communications office. Check out
  information on your diocesan website if there is
  one. The new Ecclesial movements, approved by
  the Church, are inspired by the Holy Spirit and
  are invaluable for developing a life of faith with
  other Christians.

Physical exercise plays an important part in our mental health. Find a routine of exercise that is right for you. Physical movement, including gentle walking, running, jumping, lifting weights, etc., can help to raise your mood and is good for your health too. Bring your rosary beads with you to pray as you walk.

When forgiveness is impossible

To thrive, we need to feel loved and wanted. Even though we may become God's children through baptism, the deep pain of insecurity, fuelled by anxiety or depression, can tempt us to doubt God's plan for us (see *Ep* 1:5). Childhood traumas inflicted on us by others can have a profound effect on our lives and can even be the catalyst for mental health conditions, because in some way they can rob us of hope.

The power of forgiveness can never be overestimated; it reconnects us with God and with others. God the Father of Mercies, through the death and Resurrection of his son, has sent us the Holy Spirit for the forgiveness of sins. It is by God's power over the works of Satan that forgiveness is possible. The wonderful gift of letting go of our resentment and bitterness gives us the freedom to persevere through suffering in hope. The *Our Father* reminds us that we are forgiven as we forgive others. Forgiveness brings

healing and allows us to experience the freedom that Christ has won for us (*Ga* 5:1). On the cross, Jesus neither defended himself nor felt resentment. Instead, he clung to his identity as "the Beloved" who had come from the Father and was returning to the Father. This allowed him to hand himself over to be taken, beaten, insulted, humiliated and crucified, and finally to cry out: "Father, forgive them; for they know not what they do" (*Lk* 23:34). Those who have struggled by their own efforts to forgive others for any serious pain, however, will know how hard forgiving can be.

True forgiveness is a work of the Holy Spirit, who accomplishes it in us by transforming our way of thinking: "Only the Spirit by whom we live can make 'ours' the same mind that was in Christ Jesus. Then the unity of forgiveness becomes possible and we find ourselves 'forgiving one another, as God in Christ forgave' us" (*CCC* 2842).

Forgiveness, therefore, begins with faith. One of the reasons why we are reluctant to forgive is because it means letting the offender get off without paying for what they have done to us. During the Roman Empire, crucifixion was especially cruel because its victims died slowly and in agony as a warning to others. The criminal was impaled in such a way that he had to stretch his legs to take a gulp of breath. He would writhe in agony as renewed pain would shoot through every nerve in his body. When we identify more with our pain than the desire to forgive, we merely prolong our own personal "crucifixion" caused by those who have hurt us. When Jesus let go of the debt of justice owed to him, he transformed the crucifixion into an event of love. His forgiveness was founded on his hope in the Resurrection. After his cry of abandonment (*Mt* 27:46) he prayed the following prayer of hope, silently to his Father: "Yet thou art holy, enthroned on the praises of Israel. In thee our fathers trusted; they trusted, and thou didst deliver them. To thee they cried, and were saved; in thee they trusted and were not disappointed." (*Ps* 22:3-5)

In an essay on forgiveness, the writer Henry Nouwen describes this process of forgiveness using the analogy of a dance:

> Healing begins not where our pain is taken away, but where it can be shared and seen as part of a larger pain. The first task of healing, therefore, is to take our many problems and illnesses out of their isolation and place them at the centre of the vast battle against the Evil One... As we create the space to mourn – whether through one-to-one relationships, small support groups, or communal celebrations – we free ourselves little by little from the grip of the Evil One and come to discover in the

midst of our grief that the same Spirit who calls us to mourn stirs us to make the first movement in our dance with God...

Let me describe...the movements of the dance. Let me be your dance master for a while! The first movement is forgiveness. It's a very difficult movement. But, then, all beginnings are difficult, and there is so much forgiving to do. We have to forgive our parents for not being able to give us unconditional love, our brothers and sisters for not giving us the support we dreamt about, our friends for not being there for us when we expected them. We have to forgive our church and civic leaders for their ambitions and manipulations. Beyond all that, we have to forgive all those who torture, kill, rape, destroy – who make this world such a dark place. And we, ourselves, also have to beg forgiveness. The older we become, the more clearly we see that we too, have wounded others deeply, and are part of a society of violence and destruction. It is very difficult to forgive and to ask for forgiveness. But, without this, we remain fettered to our past – unable to dance...

Forgiveness is the great spiritual weapon against the Evil One. As long as we remain victims of anger and resentment, the power of darkness can continue to divide us and tempt us with endless power games. But when we forgive those who threaten our lives, they lose their power over us... Forgiveness enables us to take the first step of the dance. (Henri J M Nouwen, *The Only Necessary Thing: Living a Prayerful Life*, 2000)

Forgiveness is possible with Jesus

There are times when we find it impossible to either forgive ourselves for something that we are ashamed of or to forgive others because of the gravity of what has been done to us. It is very common for someone who suffers from depression or anxiety to have feelings of guilt and unworthiness even though they have not necessarily committed any sins. Sin is in a sense, a declaration of independence from God: it breaks our intimacy with him and separates us from communion with others. It causes us to experience a break in our communion with the Church and the world. Pope Benedict XVI in his Encyclical Letter *Caritas in Veritate* wrote:

One of the deepest forms of poverty a person can experience is isolation. If we look closely at other kinds of poverty, including material forms, we see that they are born from isolation, from not being loved or from difficulties in being able to love. Poverty is often produced by a rejection of God's love, by man's basic and tragic tendency to close in on himself, thinking himself to be self-sufficient or merely an insignificant and ephemeral fact, a "stranger" in a random universe. Man is alienated when he is alone, when he is detached from reality, when he stops thinking and believing in a foundation… It is not by isolation that man establishes his worth, but by placing himself in relation with others and with God. (*Caritas in Veritate*, 53)

Jesus's mission of calling us out of our self-imposed loneliness into a relationship with others and with God began in Galilee with his call to repentance (*Mt* 4:17). Repentance calls us to confidence in the mercy of God. We leave our attachment to sin behind and begin taking responsibility for not making a gift of ourselves to God and to others. We turn our hearts back to God because we are tired of sin and we are drawn to him instead. As Pope Francis tells us: "When someone realises that he is a sinner and is saved by Jesus, he admits the truth to himself and discovers the hidden pearl, the buried treasure. He discovers how great life is; that there is someone who loves him so deeply that he gave his life for him." (Sergio Rubin and Francesca Ambrogetti, *Pope Francis: Conversations with Jorge Bergoglio*, 2013)

No one should ever despair of being forgiven. There is no sin which God's mercy cannot wipe clean. He forgives, without reservation, anyone who turns to him, whatever they have done. He longs for us to receive his mercy when we have turned away from him. His forgiveness produces gratitude in the hearts of those who freely accept it with an open heart. Because God's forgiveness co-operates with our freedom, we cannot experience its effects unless we receive it (see *CCC* 1864). But, as children of God in baptism, we can be confident that our Heavenly Father will forgive our sins.

However, there is a condition for receiving forgiveness: Jesus admonishes us that if we do not forgive from the heart those who have sinned against us, we too will not be forgiven. This can sound harsh for some; however, forgiveness is not about pretending that the offence never happened, or that it was no big deal – for some it can be truly grievous: the abused, the raped or mugged, those whose family members were murdered, or whose villages were exterminated in acts of genocide, etc. No one can trivialise the pain of such people. But holding on to the debt that is owed to us is like a hidden poison: it causes a cancer in our spirit through the desire for justice or revenge; it creates within us lesions of hatred and resentment and we become bound by a victim spirit that prevents us from inheriting the freedom that God wants to give us in his Kingdom. For some, therefore, unforgiveness has become a catalyst for anxiety and depression.

God's forgiveness is an enormous treasure in comparison to the value of the debt that is owed to us by others who have offended us. It is not God who withholds forgiveness from us, but rather it is we who are incapable of receiving it when our arms are too full, holding on to the toxic weight of the debt that is owed to us. By the power of his death and Resurrection, Jesus gives us the strength to let go.

Examples of those who forgave

There are many examples of men and women in the Church's history who had every reason not to forgive and yet became witnesses to the transforming power of forgiveness. The following paragraphs name but a few of them.

In 1902, eleven-year-old *Maria Goretti* died in the hospital at Nettuno, Italy, having been brutally stabbed the day before for resisting an attempted rape by a young eighteen-year-old man called Alessandro Serenelli. Before she died, however, Maria forgave her murderer. Alessandro was sentenced to thirty years in prison and was unrepentant until one night he had a dream in which Maria Goretti appeared gathering flowers and offering them to him. This experience changed him. He was released from prison after twenty-seven years and immediately went to visit Maria's mother to ask for her forgiveness. Maria Goretti was canonised in 1950.

St Maximilian Kolbe, a Catholic priest, was imprisoned in the Auschwitz concentration camp during World War II. He was housed with other prisoners, and when a small group escaped, ten men were chosen by the Germans for execution by starvation. One of the condemned men was a father of a family. Maximilian, who had not been chosen, offered himself in the man's place. Father Maximilian was the last to die: he was eventually killed by a lethal injection. He bore no malice against his executioners. He was canonised in 1982.

In 1996 seven Cistercian monks in Algeria, caught up in the Civil War, were kidnapped and murdered. One of the monks, Dom Christian de Chergé, left a moving letter, appealing for clemency for the people they loved and served, knowing that some would probably kill them.

We must remember that the witness given by these men and women comes from the fact that they forgave in Jesus Christ. None of us has the capacity to forgive from the heart by our own strength, no more than we can rise from the dead under our own power. When we engage with the grace from our baptism, we allow

the Holy Spirit to forgive for us and
of God gives us the same mind th
Jesus (see *CCC* 2842). The Sacramen
a good place to start; we should pra
sincere repentance first. To be able t
choose to allow Jesus Christ to act in us; we repent by
giving our hearts to him.

Prayer

Heavenly Father, I am sorry that I have held on to
unforgiveness; thank you for pardoning me. I place
before you all those who have hurt me – and what
they did to me. I know that by forgiving them I will
find freedom, but right now I do not have the strength
to do it. Therefore I ask you, Lord, to forgive them for
me and to allow your forgiveness to become mine.
And so, with Jesus, I forgive N. for what they did to
me, and with Jesus I cancel the debt they owe to me.
Please renew in me the healing gift of your Holy Spirit
and fill me, and all those who have hurt me, with the
Spirit of your love. Amen.

Pray the prayer *A Quarter of an Hour Before the Blessed Sacrament* to help you to forgive those who have hurt you.

- If there is someone you cannot forgive, ask God for the grace you need by making a pilgrimage to a Catholic shrine where the Sacrament of Reconciliation is usually available. Prepare yourself by praying for both the insight to know your sins and for the gift of sincere repentance. When you confess your sins, make a point of also confessing that you are holding on to the "spirit of unforgiveness".

- Find out when confessions are regularly heard in your local parish church and make an appointment with yourself to go. Do not be afraid to tell the priest if you need help in making your confession. He will listen to you without condemning you.

- Aim to go to Confession regularly, for example at least once a month, even if you do not have serious sins to confess, since the power of the sacrament will help you to stay focused on maintaining a life of grace.

When we don't have strength to carry the cross

Jesus Christ calls every Christian to follow in his footsteps – that is, to be a disciple – but with one condition: that they take up their cross and follow him (see *Mt* 16:24). For those who live with anxiety and depression, this means trusting in his power. To follow Jesus is to follow him not only to the cross but also to the Resurrection, as Bishop Fulton Sheen wrote: "Unless there is a cross in our life, there will never be an empty tomb; unless there is the crown of thorns, there will never be the halo of light." (Fulton J Sheen, *The World's First Love: Mary, Mother of God,* 1952)

The interior walls of every Catholic church generally display a series of images showing the Way of the Cross, where the events of the crucifixion of Jesus unfold. The first "station" shows Jesus presented before Pontius Pilate to be judged. He had celebrated the last supper with his Apostles the night before,

just outside the city walls of Jerusalem. They had then moved to the Garden of Gethsemane, where he agonised in prayer with the Father; and from there he was betrayed by Judas, captured by the temple guards and taken to the high priest's house to be questioned. A farcical legal process ensued, leading him to be condemned to death by crucifixion.

The important thing to notice is that in all of this Jesus was not a helpless victim (see *Mt* 26:53) – he did not offer any resistance because he wanted to identify himself with the sacrificial lambs that were being sacrificed on the same night for the Passover celebration. According to sacrificial laws, the lambs had to be perfect, without blemish and offering no resistance before being sacrificed. They played an important part in the annual memorial of the very first Passover that took place nearly a millennium and a half before: God had heard the cry of his people, held as slaves in Egypt, and he made a promise to free them and to bring them to the promised land (*Ex* 3:7-8).

On the night of the Exodus, each Hebrew family was commanded to sacrifice a lamb and to paint the lintel of the door into their houses with its blood. When the destroying angel passed over Egypt that night, the sign of the lamb's blood spared the household from death (*Ex* 12:21-27). Every firstborn male in Egypt died that night whilst every Hebrew was spared. The terrible plague gave the Hebrews their chance to flee; they escaped from slavery into freedom.

On the first Good Friday, the Blood of Jesus, the new lamb, was now to be shed as the perfect sacrifice to take away the sins of all the world, to save humanity from eternal death and to reconcile us to the Father. This paschal mystery of our liberation is at the heart of our Christian faith. It is the Good News by which we have been freed from the power of sin and death. It was at the last supper that Jesus instituted the Holy Eucharist as a lasting memorial which makes present his passion, death and Resurrection. The events that took place that first Easter were all part of the new Passover promise. His sacrifice was the only way in which the gates of heaven could be opened, to allow us to pass over with him from death to life – from slavery to freedom.

By becoming a man, God joined our humanity in its frail condition, except for sin. He was a baby that cried in a stable at Bethlehem near Jerusalem; as a boy, he was left behind in the Temple; he learnt to be a carpenter in Nazareth, and probably made a living from his work until he began his mission at the age of thirty. Jesus is one of us; but he is also the Son of God, in perfect communion with the Father. Jesus prayed to him as "Abba, Father" (*Mk* 14:36). He heard the Father call him his "beloved Son" (*Mt* 3:17) and entrusted his spirit to him when he died (*Lk* 23:46). He was sent by the Father to be his ambassador before humanity (*Jn* 14:9), and at the same time he was appointed to be our advocate with the Father (*1 Jn* 2:1), to intercede for us before his throne. In Jesus, we are reconciled to God, allowing us to share in Christ's identity and calling God "Our Father" with him. Because of this, we have the possibility of "being made partners, in a way known [only] to God, in the paschal mystery" (see *CCC* 618, citing *Gaudium et Spes* 22).

Jesus calls us to carry the cross

Jesus calls those who suffer from anxiety and depression to share in his paschal mystery by picking up their cross and following him. The mistakes and sins that we have committed can be a heavy cross to bear if they have not been transformed by faith. Looking at the remarkable life of a young American journalist, Dorothy Day, who died in 1980, we can see the power of the cross. At the age of twenty-one, she became pregnant outside of marriage and was pressured by the child's father to have an illegal abortion. She regretted the decision for the rest of her life. She was plunged into shame and depression and tried to take her own life twice. It was only when she repented and turned to the Lord for forgiveness that she found healing and could take responsibility for what she had done. The guilt of her sin became transformed into the precious cross that she would carry after the Lord as a reminder of his mercy towards her and for others. Her conversion led her to become a great advocate for the poor and marginalised of society. She went on to co-found the Catholic Workers' Movement, a collection of autonomous communities of Catholics who aim to live the gospel values of the justice and charity of Jesus, giving hospitality towards the poor.

When we embrace the very thing that crucifies us in the light of Christ's Resurrection from the dead, it can no longer crush us. Instead, it is transformed into the key ingredient for our sanctification: "[W]e rejoice in our sufferings, knowing that suffering produces endurance, and endurance produces character, and character produces hope, and hope does not disappoint us, because God's love has been poured into our hearts through the Holy Spirit who has been given to us." (*Rm* 5:3-5)

The example of St Mother Teresa

The image of the disciples of Jesus who carry their crosses and follow him is only complete when they arrive at Golgotha where Jesus was crucified. The letters of St Mother Teresa of Calcutta reveal such a disciple. The revelations of her private writings unveil a painful spiritual life. Her letters were a huge surprise for many because she was seen as a simple, happy nun, who prayed a lot and was driven to do extraordinarily good works. The reality was that she suffered from a deep hidden depression, even though she had committed her life to God. Confiding in the Archbishop of Calcutta, Ferdinand Périer, she once wrote:

> There is so much contradiction in my soul. – Such deep longing for God – so deep that it is painful – a suffering continual – and yet not wanted by God – repulsed – empty – no faith – no love – no zeal. – Souls hold no attraction – Heaven means nothing – to me it looks like an empty place – the thought of it means nothing to me and yet this torturing longing for God. – Pray for me please that I keep smiling at Him in spite of everything. For I am only His – so He has every right over me. I am perfectly happy to be nobody even to God... (Brian Kolodiejchuk, M C, *Mother Teresa: Come Be My Light: The Revealing Private Writings*)

St Mother Teresa had fallen in love with Jesus at an early age; she wanted to follow him and to be like him. The human heart, however, is incapable of containing the love that God wants to pour out into the world, and so if we are to love like him our hearts must be stretched. The more they are pulled, the larger they grow. She allowed Jesus to fill her heart with so much love that while the enlarging experience was unbearable for her, it gave incredible hope to the world. However, she did not allow herself to be a prisoner of her feelings of pain, but was guided by her faith, hope and trust in the God who was hidden from her. Her good works came from the heart of a woman who was crucified by a dark night of depression.

The cross leads us to heaven

Christ's call to carry the cross is none other than the call of every person to become like Jesus in every respect. Our Lord has opened up the possibility of transforming every illness, including anxiety and depression, into an opportunity for sanctity, by allowing us to offer it up together with his cross. Christians offer up their sufferings as a prayer for others. Through the Holy Mass, they find the Eucharistic food, the Body and Blood of Jesus, which sustains their life of grace. They identify their sufferings with Christ in the Holy Eucharist. In the Sacred Host and Chalice, we receive him both sacrificed and risen for us.

Pope St John Paul II often wrote and spoke about this vocation of every person to become holy. "Do not be afraid to be saints!" was his constant cry. In his lifetime, the Pontiff witnessed terrible sufferings: he saw his beloved Poland occupied by Nazi Germany during World War II, lost friends and family members, survived an assassination attempt, and then developed Parkinson's disease. Through all his sufferings he came to identify his life with Christ Crucified, and with the Sorrowful Mother of Jesus. Like the Beloved Disciple at the foot of the cross he offered himself as a victim out of love for others. His motto was *Totus Tuus*, meaning "everything thine", after the example of the Blessed Virgin Mary, who at the foot of the cross offered up her son, Jesus. By uniting her sorrowful heart with the offering of her son on the cross, she allowed Christ to transform her desolation into our consolation.

The example of Christ and all his suffering saints who "offer up" their pain helps us to understand the value of carrying our own cross. Their wounds became the currency of compassion, a coinage which gives meaning and value to the sufferings of others. The diocesan priest, and Doctor of the Church, St John of Ávila, speaks about this practice in a letter regarding illness:

> You may well be content to serve our Lord in illness, for when he calls people to suffer instead of working for him, he is calling them to a higher state. During our earthly exile, it is most fitting that we should carry the cross with Christ, who loved it so dearly that he chose to die on it. We can

do this better in sickness than in health, for illness is repugnant to flesh and blood and can never cause vainglory. (John of Ávila, in a letter to a layman, 1560)

Those who carry their cross to the end can hope in the consolation of eternal life. With faith as a shield against the attacks of the devil (*Ep* 6:16), those who experience anxiety, depression or both are invited to unite their suffering with the cross of Christ. In this way, their pain is transformed into a way of purification. They are also united with the Holy Souls in Purgatory. These are the men and women who died as friends of God but are in need of a time of purification. They know only too well the pain and anguish of being separated from God, but at the same time they are consoled by the knowledge that they will eventually pass through the fires of purifying love to see God's face (*CCC* 1031).

Prayer

Lord Jesus, in your name I renounce
empty promise and every temptatio
me to run away from my cross. I ask you to
from them all, and instead I offer up to you as a prayer
all my sufferings and anxieties and unite them to the
sacrifice of your cross, for those who are alone in pain
at this moment and have no one to pray for them.
I offer up my pain especially for the Holy Souls in
Purgatory who, like me, long to see your face. Amen.

Tips for carrying the cross in anxiety and depression

- Put a blessed crucifix in your room to remind you
  to think of your personal suffering joined to the
  sacrifice of Jesus on the cross.

- Imagine yourself close to Christ on the cross and
  offer up your pain with him as a "currency" for
  others who are also going through tough times, but
  have no one to pray for them.

- Keep a notebook and write in it the names of people
  you would like to pray for regularly. The very act
  of praying for others allows you to participate in
  Christ's paschal mystery.

Clinging to God in Prayer

God is passionately in love with us, and he longs for us to desire him in return. He wants to bless us and for us to know that we belong to him as his beloved sons and daughters in Jesus Christ. He also calls us to recognise that our relationship with him is frequently at risk of being sabotaged, both by our own tendencies to want to satisfy our needs (concupiscence) and by the tactics of the devil. Satan comes to steal, kill and destroy (see *Jn* 10:10). But we should not be afraid, because God does not allow us to be tempted beyond our strength (*1 Co* 10:13).

Although God never causes temptations, he allows them as a way of helping us to grow in our spiritual life; through our trials we learn to stay close to God. When we recognise both our puny limits in resisting temptations and the unparalleled strength of God, it makes sense to cling to God until he blesses us as an ally in our struggles.

The idea of holding on to God until he gives you his blessing is an iconic way of understanding prayer. It originates from a curious incident when, in the Book of Genesis, Jacob is about to confront his brother whom he had cheated in the past. There is a moment when Jacob is left alone at night and a mysterious figure appears on the scene who wrestles with Jacob until the dawn (*Gn* 32:22-31). In this struggle, Jacob recognises that he is fighting with the power of God and so he astutely clings to the stranger until God enters into an agreement with him. God does indeed want to bless the whole of humanity, but for this to happen we also need to struggle, to know our limitations and his strength. Clinging in prayer to a power greater than ourselves seems to be the most logical thing to do in the face of depression and anxiety. Pope Benedict XVI encourages us in the battle:

> Dear brothers and sisters, our entire lives are like this long night of struggle and prayer, spent in desiring and asking for God's blessing, which cannot be grabbed or won through our own strength but must be received with humility from him as a gratuitous gift that ultimately allows us to recognise the Lord's face. And when this happens, our entire reality changes; we receive a new name and God's blessing. (Pope Benedict XVI, General Audience, Wednesday 25th May 2011)

We are never alone in prayer

Prayer is never an individual experience. The *Our Father* teaches us that we belong to a family that has God as its Father. We are brothers and sisters in Christ. From the very beginning, men and women have naturally prayed to God as they searched for him as their creator, but it is through Abraham that prayer is first revealed to us in the Bible. He shows us that when we habitually submit our hearts to God in prayer, our minds gradually become conformed to his to the point that we forget ourselves and begin to see the world as he does.

Like all the great men and women of the Old Testament, from Abraham to Elijah, those who encounter God somehow grow to become like Jesus Christ in his mission of intercession for God's people. His ultimate prayer was to offer himself on the cross for humanity. In this light, it is possible even to offer the very experience of depression and anxiety as a prayer of intercession for the world. As members of the Church, every Christian who suffers from a mental health condition is called to be a disciple of Jesus, to pick up their cross and to follow him, but we cannot do this unless we have a relationship with him through prayer.

Prayer is essential

A regular prayer life is essential for finding God as a help in anxiety and depression. However, for anyone who finds it impossible to get out of bed in the morning, the last thing they may feel like doing is to get on their knees and pray. The fact is, anyone who engages in praying will always come across obstacles. Discouraging experiences in prayer – of dryness and distractions, sadness and disappointments, misunderstandings and so on – can lead anyone to conclude that prayer is a waste of time and so to want to give up. But God calls us to waste our time with him! When we cry out to God for help, from a place of deep pain, we may feel that we are not being heard. We may find ourselves asking: "Where is God, why has he abandoned me?" But those who persevere, and plough on with regular prayer, regardless of how they feel, grow in holiness, in patience and, most importantly, in peace.

Peace does not mean the absence of pain, but rather the acceptance of our situation. People will always pray to God in times of crises. Even those who have never prayed in their lives can find themselves on their knees as a last resort, praying with all their might and making all kinds of promises to be a better person, if only God would help them "right now".

We can even spend the whole night, in desperation, praying for an impossible intention. However, if we have never actually learnt how to pray we may think that the best part of an hour has been spent in prayer, whereas, in fact, we have simply spent sixty minutes, pacing up and down or on our knees, panicking and worrying.

Another common mistake is to treat prayer as a relaxation technique with the goal of avoiding the cross by "emptying the mind". Prayer techniques based on New Age spiritualities such as yoga and reiki are increasingly being offered, even in churches and schools. These should be avoided, because they do not flow from the Christian tradition handed down to us from Jesus and his Apostles and therefore can even be harmful to those who are already spiritually vulnerable (see Pontifical Councils for Culture and Interreligious Dialogue, *Jesus Christ, the Bearer of the Water of Life: A Christian Reflection on the "New Age"*, 2002).

The experience of prayer

St John Damascene described prayer as "the raising of one's mind and heart to God or the requesting of good things from God" (*CCC* 2559). Prayer does not have to be complicated. However, there is an order and purpose to prayer that we need to allow the Holy Spirit to teach us (*CCC* 2650). The Christian tradition of prayer, revealed to us in the Bible, has a definite form to it. It can be described in five ways (*CCC* 2626-2643):

1. Blessing and adoring God
2. Petitioning God
3. Interceding on behalf of others
4. Thanking God
5. Praising God.

We also come to prayer through the theological virtues of faith, hope and love in Jesus Christ and we listen attentively to God speaking to us through the events of our daily life. We allow Christ to speak to us through the Word of God in the Bible and through the formal times of prayer and worship (liturgy) in our churches where the people of God come to gather, such as the Holy Mass, Morning and Evening Prayer, Adoration and Benediction, etc. We pray in the name of Jesus, to the Father, in the Holy Spirit. We pray in communion with the holy Mother of God, as the mother of Jesus and our mother, given to us at the foot of the cross. (*CCC* 2673-2679). Lastly, we pray in three different ways: with our voices (vocal), using our thoughts and reflections (meditative), and through inner prayer (contemplative) (*CCC* 2700-2719).

Vocal prayer involves using bodily gestures, music and art to give expression to our thoughts towards God. We pray out loud before meals, at Mass or in Christian support groups, etc.

Meditative prayer involves using the Bible and inspired writing from the tradition of the Church. For example, we carefully "chew" over what we have read, thinking about how it applies to our lives. Spiritual reading feeds our prayer life, as do holy icons and music. We try to "listen" to what the Lord is saying to us through these things.

Contemplative prayer or inner prayer is in some ways the simplest because we do not need to do anything, except to be alone in silence with God; yet at the same time, it is not the easiest expression of prayer. This kind of prayer can be done at any time, even when a person struggles to get out of bed. Through inner prayer, we inevitably face dryness and distractions that can make us want to give up praying altogether! There is no technique for contemplative prayer; "it is a gift, a grace", which has to be accepted "in humility and poverty". For some, contemplative prayer can be the most intense form of prayer through which the Lord works at a deep level within our hearts.

The Gospel of Luke teaches us that prayer requires us to learn how to persist and not give up (*CCC* 2613), like an importunate friend who knocks on his neighbour's door for bread or like the persistent widow who continues to ask for justice from an unjust judge against her enemy, believing that she will get it. We must also grow in humility and sincerity before God, like the tax collector in Luke's Gospel who beat his breast, praying "God, be merciful to me a sinner!"

Our life of prayer is not meant to simply build ourselves up. It is given to us as a gift to nourish our missionary life. The Apostles were called by the Lord, they followed Jesus and betrayed him, but it was not until they experienced him as the Risen and Ascended Lord that they really knew him. It was then that they were empowered in their relationship with God and received his nature as sons of God in communion with the Father.

In the Gospels, everyone who was either sick or demonised was healed or delivered on meeting Jesus Christ. Although, by the Gospel accounts, none of the Apostles needed physical healing, those who witnessed his Resurrection were cured of a deeper illness of fear and incredulity. Like the Apostles, those who suffer from anxiety and depression need to receive the hope of eternal life if they are to be effective witnesses of the gospel. Today, just as in his lifetime, many people have met Jesus, but they have not become his disciples, only because they did not accept his authority. Those who do accept him as Lord are set alight with his love and are commissioned to share in the task of bringing about the Kingdom of God on earth as it is in heaven. Saint Josemaría Escrivá, echoing Saint Cyprian, taught that "[e]mbracing the Christian faith means committing oneself to continuing Jesus Christ's mission among men. We must, each of us, be *alter Christus, ipse Christus*: another Christ, Christ himself" (*Christ is Passing By: Homilies by Josemaría Escrivá*).

It is by the gift of the Holy Spirit that we become true apostles in the world. He is given to all those who pray. If you find that you have no energy to pray or if your thoughts are distracted by anxiety, then setting aside time for prayer and sticking to it is the best way to make sure that you pray regularly even when you do not feel like it. The Church has a natural rhythm of prayer time, and has different types of prayer, designed for all the faithful to take part in. These include Mass on Sundays and holy days of obligation; regular time spent reading the Bible; the Rosary; Adoration of the Blessed Sacrament; and other devotions that can help us to be focused on the Lord's power over our struggles.

Difficulties in Prayer

Distractions are a natural part of our struggle to pray. They help us to see where our heart lies and can call us to turn back to God each time. The battle of prayer means that every time we are conscious of any distractions, we choose to let them go. If we spend an hour distracted in prayer, and every thirty seconds we choose to turn our minds back to God, it means that we develop the habit of putting God first every time. Prayer is difficult. It requires effort. For some, it would be "nice" if we could be filled with all the benefits of prayer without the struggle – a bit like having a fabulous body without worrying about eating too many calories or exercising. But the very struggle in prayer is necessary because by it we learn how to depend on God.

When our first parents, Adam and Eve, were tempted into disobeying God, sin entered the world for the first time (Original Sin) and it has been handed down to us through every generation (*Gn* 3:1-7). Since we have all inherited Original Sin we struggle against ourselves and against our laziness, our moods and our disordered appetites. The trials and temptations sent by the devil also tempt us away from union with God. But our struggle in prayer stretches us. God's greatest desire for humanity is to bless us through our relationship of prayer with him. However, God will not impose himself on us; our hearts must be open to receive his grace. Anyone who has tried to pray in earnest will know about the challenges that face us: distractions; boredom; racing thoughts; and spiritual laziness. In moments when it seems that you have no strength to read the Bible or to pray the Rosary or other prayers that use a lot of words, it is always possible to cry out to God with the simplest prayer: "Help me!"

Feeling unworthy to pray

The foundation of prayer is humility. It means that we come to God knowing who we are: through baptism, we are God's beloved children who depend on him for our existence. To think of ourselves as anything else comes from pride. It does not mean that we are perfect; far from it. At times, our identity as God's children is tarnished because of the battles that we have engaged in through temptation. Humility also accepts that God wants to spend time with us, no matter what terrible things we may have done or said, or dreadful thoughts we have had, or things we have failed to do! He longs for us to return to him when we have strayed far away from him. In a sense, we can say that God thirsts for us; he wants us to need him so that he can pour out his graces into our hearts (*CCC* 2567). It is entirely possible that depression, anxiety, or both disorders together can lead someone to think that they should not pray because they are unworthy. However, the experience of the Church is that we should pray precisely because we are unworthy. In the book *The Way of a Pilgrim*, written by an unknown nineteenth-century Russian peasant, we come across a traveller who suffers from depression and anxiety. He feels unworthy to pray because he mistakenly believes that he must earn God's love. The advice given to him can apply to anyone who finds it difficult to pray from a spirit of unworthiness:

> Beloved brother, in your fear and dejection you should pray to God; prayer is the primary form of healing of all our troubles. "But I cannot pray," he said to me. "I think that the moment that I begin to pray God will destroy me." Nonsense, brother! Such thoughts are from the evil one. God is infinitely merciful and sympathises with the sinner; He is eager to forgive anyone who repents. If you know the Jesus Prayer, that is 'Lord Jesus Christ, have mercy on me a sinner,' then say it without ceasing. (*The Way of a Pilgrim: And the Pilgrim Continues His Way*)

On the same subject, St Louis De Montfort exhorts those who feel unworthy to pray the Rosary not to give up praying:

I have just said that to say the Rosary to advantage one must be in a state of grace "or at least be fully determined to give up mortal sin;" first of all, because, if it were true that God only heard the prayers of those in a state of grace it would follow that people in a state of mortal sin should not pray at all. This is an erroneous teaching which has been condemned by Holy Mother Church, because of course sinners need to pray far more than good people do. Were this horrible doctrine true it would then be useless and futile to tell a sinner to say all, or even part of his Rosary, because it would never help him. (St Louis De Montfort, *The Secret of the Rosary*)

Prayer of the heart

When negative thoughts begin to overwhelm us, it is important not to engage with them. The majority of these ideas are based on lies and deceptions about our relationship with God and our neighbour. The best way to combat these kinds of thoughts is by trusting in the power of the name of Jesus. Miracles have been worked in his name. By getting into the habit of occupying our thoughts with the Lord's name we can put up a strong wall of defence against our damaging ideas. The Jesus Prayer is a spiritual discipline which takes its initiative from one of the shortest verses in the New Testament. Here St Paul exalts us to "pray constantly" (*1 Th* 5:17). It consists of repeatedly calling on the name of Jesus by just repeating the prayer "Lord Jesus have mercy on me a sinner."

The aim of the prayer is not to empty the mind, but rather to quieten it by focusing on the name of Jesus. It means that all the distractions and images that come to us during our quiet moments are put to one side. The prayer does require perseverance and commitment, because it soon becomes apparent that the imagination is full of distracting thoughts, jumping up and down, trying to attract our attention. The prayer is said sitting still and is repeated, slowly. Any images or thoughts that do come to mind are set gently aside, without panic, as one returns to the prayer for the duration of the time we have given over to it. By repeatedly calling on the name of Jesus without ceasing the Prayer of the Heart allows God to speak to us at a deep level. The prayer is described here in more detail:

> Sit alone and in silence; bow your head and close your eyes; relax your breathing and with your imagination look into your heart; direct your thoughts from your head into your heart. And while inhaling say, "Lord Jesus Christ, have mercy on me," either softly with your lips or in your mind. Endeavour to

fight distractions but be patient and peaceful and repeat this process frequently. (*The Way of a Pilgrim: And the Pilgrim Continues His Way*)

By clinging to God in prayer, those who suffer from an anxiety disorder, depression or both will find God as an ally. Like Jacob who wrestled with an angel, the Lord invites us to persevere in prayer and in faith. If we hold on, he will give us his blessing!

Prayer

Heavenly Father, I am sorry for engaging with negative thoughts about myself. I accept the gift of your forgiveness over me. Through the Precious Blood of your Son, Jesus Christ, drive far away from me every attack of the Evil One and pour out upon me the gift of your Holy Spirit. Fill every area of my life that is empty with the divine fire of your love, through Christ our Lord. Amen.

Tips for praying in anxiety and depression

- If you are not used to praying, begin by asking Jesus to come into your heart. Speak to him using your own words, as you would a friend. The Rosary is the best prayer to learn first of all, since you will have a great help in the Virgin Mary.

- Make a basic plan for your day the night before. Develop a manageable routine of prayer that will carry you and stick to it! Use already established key moments such a meal times or brushing your teeth to anchor your prayer routine.

- Use Gregorian chant, or Christian praise and worship music in prayer. It worked for King David! (see *1 S* 16:23). Listening to inspired music can even help in getting to sleep.

- Set up a prayer space or corner. Furnish it with a Bible, a crucifix and an image of Our Lady. Make it the focal point of your personal prayer life.

Prayers

The Lord has assured us that when we pray to him, we will find him (*Mt* 7:7-8). The following is a brief selection of prayers which can be useful in the search for God through anxiety and depression. If you are not used to praying, it is suggested that you find a quiet place to pray where you will not be interrupted.

A Quarter of an Hour Before the Blessed Sacrament

To please, Me, dear child, it is not necessary to know much; all that is required is to love Me much, to be deeply sorry for ever having offended Me and desirous of being ever faithful to Me in future.

Speak to Me now as you would do to your dearest friend. Tell Me all that now fills your mind and heart. Are there any you wish to commend to Me? Tell Me their names, and tell Me what you would wish Me to do for them. Do not fear, ask for much; I love generous hearts, which, forgetting themselves, wish well to others.

Speak to Me of the poor you wish to comfort; tell Me of the sick you would wish to see relieved. Ask of Me something for those who have been unkind to you, or who have crossed you. Ask much for them all; commend them with all your heart to Me.

And ask Me many graces for yourself. Are there not many graces you would wish to name that would make you happier in yourself, more useful and pleasing to others, more worthy of the love of Me, the dearest Lord, Master, and Spouse of your soul? Tell Me the whole list of the favours you want of Me, tell Me them with humility, knowing how poor you are without them, how unable to gain them by yourself; ask for them with much love, that they may make you more pleasing to Me. With all a child's simplicity, tell Me how self-seeking you are, how proud, vain, irritable, how cowardly in sacrifice, how lazy in work, uncertain in your good resolutions, and then ask Me to bless and crown your efforts. Poor child, fear not, blush not at the sight of so many failings; there are saints in heaven who had the faults you have; they came to Me lovingly, they prayed earnestly to Me and My grace has made them good and holy in My sight.

You should be Mine, body and soul; fear not, therefore to ask of Me gifts of body and mind, health, judgement, memory, and success – ask for them for My sake; that God may be glorified in all things. I can grant everything, and never refuse to give what may make a soul dearer to Me and better able to fulfil the will of God. Have you no plans for the future which occupy, perhaps distress, your mind? Tell Me your hopes, your fears. Is it about your future state? Your position among My creatures? Some good you wish to bring to others? In what shall I help and bless your good will?

And for me you must – have you not? – some zeal, some wish to do good to the souls of others. Some, perhaps, who love and care for you, have ceased, almost to know or care for Me. Shall I give you strength, wisdom and tact, to bring these poor ones close to My heart again? Have you failed in the past? Tell Me how you acted; I will show you why you did not gain all you expected; rely on Me, I will help you, and will guide you to lead others to Me.

And what crosses have you, My dear child? Have they been many and heavy ones? Has someone caused you pain? Did someone wound your self-love? Slighted you? Injured you? Lay your head upon My breast, and tell Me how you suffered. Have you felt that some have been ungrateful to you, and unfeeling towards you? Tell Me all, and in the warmth of My heart, you will find the strength to forgive and even to forget that they have ever wished to pain you.

And what fears have you, My child? My providence shall comfort you, My love sustain you. I am never away from you, never can abandon you. Are some growing cold in the interest and love they had for you? Pray to Me for them; I will restore them to you if it be better for you and your sanctification.

Have you got some happiness to make known to Me? What has happened since you came to Me last, to console you, to gladden and give you joy? What was it? A mark of true friendship you received? A success unexpected and almost unhoped for? A fear suddenly taken away from you? And did you remember the while, that in all it was My will, My love, that brought all that your heart has been so glad to have? It was My hand, My dear child, that guided and prepared all for you. Look to Me now, My child, and say: "Dear Jesus, I thank You."

You will soon leave Me now; what promises can you make Me? Let them be sincere ones, humble ones, full of love and desire to please Me. Tell Me how carefully you will avoid every occasion of sin, drive from you all that leads to harm, and shun the world – the great deceiver of souls. Promise to be kind to the poor; loving, for My sake, to friends; forgiving to your enemies, and charitable to all, not in word alone and actions, but in your very thoughts. When you have little love for your neighbour, whom you see, you are forgetting Me who am hidden from you.

Love all My Saints; seek the help of your holy patrons. I love to glorify them by giving you much through them. Love, above all, My own sweet glorious Mother – she is your mother; love her, speak to her often, and she will bring you to Me, and for her sake, I will love and bless you more each day.

Return soon to Me again, but come with your heart empty of the world, for I have many more favours to give, more than you can know of; bring your heart so that I may fill it with many gifts of My love.

My peace be with you.

Prayer of the Apostle Philip

Jesus, I surrender to You.
I thank You that Your life reveals to me
the home that my heart is searching for.
Following You, my heart is stirred with passion
to see the Father, to know Him as You do.
Because of You, God is my Father.
Standing with Your Apostle Philip,
I now say with my whole heart:
Lord, show me the Father, and I shall be satisfied.
I am grateful beyond words
that You have come to reveal Him to me.
(From Neal Lozano, Matthew Lozano, John Eldredge
and John Horn, *Abba's Heart: Finding Our Way Back
to the Father's Delight*)

Novena Prayer to Our Lady, Untier of Knots

Holy Mary, full of God's presence during the days
   of your life,
you accepted with full humility the Father's will,
and the devil was never capable of entangling you
   with his confusion.
Once with your son you interceded
   for our difficulties,
and, full of kindness and patience,
   you set us an example
of how to untie the knots in our lives.
And by remaining forever our Mother,
you put in order, and make clearer,
   the ties that link us to the Lord.
Holy Mother, Mother of God, and our Mother,
we ask you, who untie with motherly heart the
   knots of our lives,
to receive into your hands [name of person]
and free him/her of the knots and confusion
   with which our enemy attacks.
Through your grace, your intercession,
   and your example,
deliver us from all evil, Our Lady,
   and untie the knots
that prevent us from being united with God,
so that we, free from sin and error,
may find Him in all things,

may have our hearts placed in Him,
and may serve Him always in our brothers
and sisters. Amen.
(Mario H Ibertis Rivera (VMS))

The Memorare

Remember, O most gracious Virgin Mary, that never
was it known that anyone who fled to thy protection,
implored thy help, or sought thy intercession, was left
unaided. Inspired by this confidence I fly unto thee,
O Virgin of virgins, my Mother. To thee do I come,
before thee I stand, sinful and sorrowful. O Mother of
the Word Incarnate, despise not my petitions, but in
thy mercy hear and answer me. Amen.

Jesus Help Me

Jesus help me, your servant whom you have
    redeemed by your Precious Blood.
In every need let me come to you
    with humble trust, saying: Jesus help me.
In all my doubts, perplexities and temptations:
    Jesus help me.
In hours of loneliness, weariness and trial:
    Jesus help me.
In the failure of my plans and hopes:
    Jesus help me.
In disappointments, troubles and sorrows:
    Jesus help me.

When I throw myself on your tender love
  as a Father and a Saviour: Jesus help me.
When I feel impatient and my cross is heavy:
  Jesus help me.
When I am ill, and my head and hands cannot
  do their work: Jesus help me.
Always, always, in joys or sorrows,
  in falls and shortcomings: Jesus help me. Amen.
(William G Storey, *Prayers of Christian Consolation*)

Morning Offering

O my God, I offer you all my thoughts,
  words, actions and sufferings;
and I beseech you to give me your grace that
  I may not offend you this day
but may faithfully serve you and do your holy will
  in all things.
I entrust myself completely to your boundless
  mercy today and always.

O Lord, you have brought me to the beginning
  of a new day.
Save me by your power so that I may not fall
  into any sin.
May everything I say, and all that I do,
be directed to the performance of your justice,
through Christ our Lord.

Lord, may everything I do
   begin with your inspiration,
continue with your help and reach conclusion
   under your guidance. Amen.

A Short Night Prayer

In your mercy, Lord,
dispel the darkness of this night.
Let your household so sleep in peace
that at the dawn of a new day
they may, with joy, waken in your name.
Through Christ our Lord,
Amen.
(Taken from the Divine Office,
Compline for Tuesday Night)

The Divine Mercy Prayer

Jesus, I trust in You!

The Jesus Prayer

Lord Jesus, be merciful to me a sinner.

Useful resources

Catholic resources:

- **The Catholic Bishops' Conference of England and Wales** [Providing information about the Catholic Church in the England and Wales] (*www.cbcew.org.uk*)

- **Catholic Mental Health Project** [A Catholic organisation offering advice and support for those suffering from mental health issues. Telephone: 07581 205314. Postal address: Catholic Mental Health Project, Department for Christian Responsibility and Citizenship, Catholic Bishops' Conference of England and Wales, 39 Eccleston Square, London SW1V 1BX] (*www.catholicmentalhealthproject. org.uk*)

- **The Dympna Centre** [A Catholic counselling service for clergy and religious. Phone: 01423 817515. Postal address: Parkside House, 17 East Parade, Harrogate HG1 5LF] (*www.thedympnacentre. co.uk*)

Non-Catholic resources:

- **Samaritans** [A UK charity that offers a safe and confidential 24-hour listening ear for any problems. Phone: 116 123. Postal address: Freepost RSRB-KKBY-CYJK, PO Box 9090, Stirling, FK8 2SA. Email: jo@samaritans.org] (*www.samaritans.org*)

- **Anxiety UK** [A UK charity that offers support and advice to those suffering with anxiety disorders. It also operates a helpline, staffed by volunteers with personal experience of anxiety. Phone: 08444 775 774 (Mon–Fri: 9.30 a.m.–5.30 p.m.)] (*www.anxietyuk.org.uk*)

- **The Mental Health Foundation** [A British Charity providing information and helpful resources on mental health problems. It carries out research, and campaigns to improve services for affected people.](*www.mentalhealth.org.uk*)

- **Saneline** [A helpline offering specialist emotional support and information to anyone affected by mental illness, including family, friends and carers. Phone: 0845 767 8000 (every day 6 p.m.–11 p.m.)](*www.sane.org.uk*)

- **Association of Christian Councillors** [A professional body set up in 1992 to facilitate quality counselling, psychotherapy, pastoral care and related training] (*www.acc-uk.org*)

- **Association for Post Natal Illness** [Offers information as a network of volunteers with experience of postnatal illness. It operates a telephone helpline. Phone: 020 7386 0868 (Mon–Fri: 10.00 a.m.–2.00 p.m.)] (*www.apni.org*)

- **Alcoholics Anonymous** [A charity that offers fellowship to men and women in finding hope and help to recover from alcoholism. Phone: 0845 769 7555] (*www.alcoholics-anonymous.org.uk*)

- **EmotionsAnonymous** [Following the 12-Step program of recovery. The website is based in the US and provides information on where meetings are held around the world, including in the UK.] (*www.emotionsanonymous.org*)

- **Rethink Mental Illness** [A British mental health charity providing practical advice on living with mental illness. Phone: 0300 5000 927 (Mon–Fri: 9.30 a.m.–4 p.m.)] (*www.rethink.org*)

Bibliography

Catechism of the Catholic Church (Burns & Oates, 2011).

Catholic Bishops' Conference of England and Wales, *Cherishing Life* (CTS & Colloquium (CaTEW) Ltd, 2004).

Cantalamessa, Raniero, *Life in Christ: The Spiritual Message of the Letter to the Romans* (Collegeville, Minnesota: The Liturgical Press, 1997).

Ciszek, Walter J (foreword) and Bacovcin, Helen (transl.), *The Way of a Pilgrim: And the Pilgrim Continues His Way* (Image Classics, 1978).

Ellsberg, Robert (ed.), *All the Way to Heaven: The Selected Letters of Dorothy Day* (Milwaukee: Marquette University Press, 2010).

Escrivá, Josemaría, *Christ is Passing By: Homilies by Josemaría Escrivá* (Dublin: Four Courts Press, 1982).

Kheriaty, Aaron, MD, *The Catholic Guide to Depression* (Manchester, New Hampshire, USA: Sophia Institute Press, 2012).

Kolodiejchuk, Brian, M C, *Mother Teresa: Come Be My Light: The Revealing Private Writings* (Rider, 2008).

Lozano, Neal, *Unbound: A Practical Guide to Deliverance* (Chosen Books, 2003).

Lozano, Neal, Lozano, Matthew, Eldredge, John and Horn, John, *Abba's Heart: Finding Our Way Back to the Father's Delight* (Chosen Books, 2015).

Nouwen, Henri J M, *The Only Necessary Thing: Living a Prayerful Life* (Darton Longman & Todd, 2000).

Pontifical Councils for Culture and Interreligious Dialogue, *Jesus Christ, the Bearer of the Water of Life: A Christian Reflection on the "New Age"* (2002).

Pope Paul VI, *Gaudium et Spes: Pastoral Constitution on the Church in the Modern World* (1965).

Rubin, Sergio and Ambrogetti, Francesca, *Pope Francis: Conversations with Jorge Bergoglio* (Putnam, 2013).

Sherriff , G B (Rev. Bro.), *Courage and a Man's Part* (Australian CTS, Pamphlet No. 1457, 1965).

De Montfort, St Louis, *The Secret of the Rosary* (Charlotte, North Carolina: TAN Books, 1987).

De Montfort, St Louis, *True Devotion to Mary: With Preparation for Total Consecration* (Catholic Way Publishing, 2012).

Kowlaska, St Maria Faustina, *Divine Mercy in My Soul: Diary of Saint Maria Faustina Kowalska* (Stockbridge: Marian Press, 2005).

Storey, William G, *Prayers of Christian Consolation* (Chicago: Loyola Press, 2008).